Peter Reading was born in 1946  Art at the Liverpool College of History of Art. He has also been Residence at Sunderland Polyte won many awards, including the Cholmondeley Award for Poetry (1978), the Dylan Thomas Award (1983) and the Whitbread Poetry Prize (1986). He was elected a Fellow of the Royal Society of Literature in 1988.

LAST POEMS

LAST POEMS

Peter Reading

Chatto & Windus
LONDON

First published in Great Britain in 1994

1 3 5 7 9 10 8 6 4 2

© Peter Reading 1994

Peter Reading has asserted his right under the
Copyright, Designs and Patents Act, 1988 to be
identified as the author of this work

Published in 1994 by
Chatto & Windus Limited
Random House, 20 Vauxhall Bridge Road
London SW1V 2SA

Random House Australia (Pty) Limited
20 Alfred Street, Milsons Point, Sydney,
New South Wales 2061, Australia

Random House New Zealand Limited
18 Poland Road, Glenfield
Auckland 10, New Zealand

Random House South Africa (Pty) Limited
PO Box 337, Bergvlei, South Africa

Random House UK Limited Reg. No. 954009

A CIP catalogue record for this book is available from
the British Library

ISBN 0 7011 6100 0

Typeset by SX Composing Ltd, Rayleigh, Essex
Printed in Great Britain by
Mackays of Chatham PLC, Chatham, Kent

This book was completed with the assistance of an award from the
Authors' Foundation.

The two poems entitled 'Ovidian' were commissioned by Michael
Hofmann and James Lasdun for *Ovid's Metamorphoses*,
Faber & Faber 1994

To Deborah *née* Jackson

Contents

Foreword

These poems are printed in the order in which they were found (contained in an envelope bearing a superscription, in the author's hand, 'Last Poems', together with a holograph note indicating that the pieces 'Euripidean' and 'Thucydidean' should be ascribed to 'an anonymous cleric of the nineteenth century').

The sanguinary 'Ovidian' is a treatment, in two parts, of Ovid's *Metamorphoses* (IV. 663-803 and V. 1-235) done into Reading's characteristic quasi-classical hexameters. 'Homeric' is an adaptation, similarly rendered, of XXII. 381-477 from the *Odyssey*.

The poems entitled 'Funerary', 'Fragmentary' and 'Exilic' are evidently 'versions' of Anglo-Saxon pieces (respectively, the end of *Beowulf*, 'The Ruin' and 'The Wife's Lament'). 'Fates of Men' derives from a poem of that title in the *Exeter Book*.

'Erosive' and the untitled final two pages are reproduced as found. It is unclear whether the author intended them to appear in their present form, or whether they represent drafts towards an unrealized work in progress.

John Bilston, Melaleuca, 1994.

[UNTITLED]

[wizened anhydrous frail wisps of laurel leaves,
rustle of old gratuitous scrivening,
pages of faded palimpsest hieroglyphs,
half-hidden/half-glimpsed sorrowful utterance,
sepia faded tremulous holograph,
crackle of brittle anhydrous laurel leaves,
sepia-scrivened crumbled eroded leaves,
parchment eroded round the sad utterance,
rotted the frail bond, with it the utterance,]

FUNERARY

Preparing a pyre,   the people of the Geats
hung round it helmets,   halberds and battle-dress;
lamenting, they laid   their lord in the midst of it.
High on the wold   his warriors kindled it,
wood-smoke whirled,   there was weeping, flames leapt.
After the wind's-rush,   the white-hot cadaver
fell into fragments.   Fear was expressed
by a Geatish woman   who wailed a keen
over the body,   bad times were forecast –
terror, killing,   captivity, shame.
The smoke was swallowed   by sky. On the headland
a barrow was built,   both broad and lofty,
a landmark for miles   to mariners. Ten days
later they finished it,   a fine memorial
for a man so mighty   in martial conflict.
A vault was wrought   around his ashes.
Trappings, taken   from the treasure-hoard, next were
buried in the barrow –   bright gold entrusted
to earth, where it rests,   rusted, useless
as all world's-gear is.   Geatish princes
rode round the mound,   making great grief.

And this is fitting: for fair men to value
with powerful words   their worthy lord
when his life, as all men's   must, departs him.
So the men of the Geats,   Great-Hall-dwellers,
who'd shared the hearth   with the hero, bewailed,
claiming their king   was the kindest of leaders,
the mildest of men,   most meriting renown.

REGAL

Mother was holding up a Pyrex pie-dish
(lined with plump apple lumps) in her left hand,
flopping the pastry lid on with her right,
trimming the droopy overlaps and jabbing
steam-vents. She wiped a floured hand on her apron
and tuned the wireless – what Roy Fuller calls
'Some inexplicable, imperial,
Elgarian sadness' filled the scullery:
His Majesty, King George VI, is dead.

The following year we single-filed from school
down to the flicks to see a double feature
(stark Everest surmounted by Tenzing,
and the Queen crowned). The Regal, I recall,
was gaudy, faded, had seen better days.

EURIPIDEAN

What we have long foretold will before long be
    fully accomplished, the theme of dirges.

Low, low it lies, imperial majesty,
vanished the pomp, the high-vaunted vanities,
    nothing remains, no name, no issue.

Mothers, expire with grief on beholding your
progeny thus deformed and your lovely ones
    now become loathsome, pallid, death-waxed.

    Hostile manipulator, Cronus,
    what need had I of sons or daughters?
This grievous fate should not have befallen me:
    children from these arms wrenched for ever.

    Not to be borne, such weight of anguish.

See, the audacious miscreants suffering.

'Wretch that I am! What cause is assignable
for such a chain of diresome calamities?'
Folly, towards which untutored man inclines;
    Sunk City's scum and pestilential
terrors, ascribe to gods unassuageable.

Nor may we now reach forth with our impotent
    hands to forestall our headlong downrush,
    having irrevocably acted.

    Some, there are, hold that the ills attending
    mankind exceed his joys; per contra,
others opine that his frail life encompasses
more bliss than woe – for how could he, otherwise,
    bear to endure each grief-racked orbit?

BOSNIAN

Sipping grit-coffee and vinjak outside a
    bar in the Turkish
Quarter, observe how Hooded Crows crowd and
    bicker for carrion
in the fast-darkening air grown rank with
    barbecued lambs' smoke.

(Sarajevo, 1992)

HOMERIC

After Odysseus had slaughtered the Suitors he
  grimly surveyed them –
sprawling in crans in a welter of blood and
  muck, like the beached fish
dragged up by driftnetters onto the sand to
  gulp for the grey brine
till in the heat of the sun they expire, so
  lay the slain Suitors.

Calling Telemachus, devious-thinking
  wily Odysseus
asked for the nurse Eurycleia to be brought
  into his presence.

Rattling her door, Telemachus shouted
  old Eurycleia,
matron in charge of the servant women, to
  go to his father.

When she arrived, she discovered Odysseus
  striding through corpses,
spattered with offal and gore, like a lion
  leaving a farmstead
where he has feasted on cattle, the blood-gouts
  staining his body.

When she set eyes on the dead and the blood-bath,
  old Eurycleia
let out a triumphal yell but Odysseus
  stopped her with these words:
'Silence, old woman, for it is immoral to
  gloat over slain men;
justice was meted out to them by the
  gods for their evil,
they have been slain for their want of respect, their
  doom has been dreadful.

Now, let us talk of the women attendants –
   who has betrayed me?'
'Sir, of the fifty who serve in your household
   twelve should be punished
for their recalcitrance – even Penelope
   couldn't control them.'
'Go to those women who flouted decorum;
   summon them to me.'
These were his words, and the nurse was quick to
   muster the culprits.

Meanwhile Odysseus briefed his son and his
   two faithful herdsmen:
'Carry the carcasses out of here – order the
   women to help you.
Then swab the elegant chairs and tables with
   sponges and water.
Then, when the palace is cleansed and in order,
   take out the women,
lead them between the domed outhouse and the
   wall of the courtyard,
then with your long-bladed swords make sure you
   hack them to pieces –
end their lascivious memories of lewd
   nights with the Suitors.'

Howling, convulsively sobbing, the women were
   herded together.
Firstly they dragged out the carcasses, dumped them
   under the portal
(superintending, Odysseus forced their
   unwilling labour);
next, they attended to swabbing the elegant
   chairs and the tables;
meanwhile Telemachus worked with the pair of
   trustworthy herdsmen
scraping with shovels the crusted blood-clots

out of the flooring,
ordered the women to carry away the
   loathsome detritus.

Now that the palace was cleansed and in order, the
   women were taken,
herded between the domed outhouse and the
   wall of the courtyard,
into a corner from which there could be no
   hope of escaping.
Worthy Telemachus next outlined his
   plan of disposal:
'Death by the sword is too good for these sluts who
   brought to this household
shameful dishonour and sully us by their
   wanton cavortings.'
Seizing a hawser, removed from the deck of some
   blue-prowed vessel,
ever-resourceful Telemachus lashed it
   high on a column,
slung it across the dome of the outhouse,
   tautened it so that
anyone strung from it wouldn't be able to
   reach for a foothold.
Then, in the same way as thrushes or doves dropping
   into a thicket,
seeking a roosting-place, find only snares set
   cruelly to kill them,
so did the women, their heads in a row of
   tightly-drawn nooses,
dangle and writhingly twitch until death had
   stilled their convulsions.

Next, through the gate they dragged the treacherous
   goatherd Melanthius
[trussed, he had been, by the hands and feet and
   roped to a roof-beam,

left there suspended and suffering since the
  heat of the battle].
Plying a keen-edged blade, they sawed his
  nose and his ears off,
carved off his genitals, tossed them aside as
  meat for the mongrels.
Finally, hacking his hands and his feet off, their
  fury was sated.

FATES OF MEN

Many children are fathered,   fondled by parents,
fostered, sent forth;   but Fate is impartial:

maybe a man dies   mauled in his youth
by wandering wolves,   the wily heath-dwellers;
for some folk, famine   finishes all things;
hurricanes hurl   much hardship on one man;
ash-spears may bloody him;   the battlefield fell him;
one may go blundering,   blindness afflicting him;
another is lamed,   his leg's bones sundered
so that he moans,   menaced by Fate's lot;
one, forced to wander,   wearies of foreigners –
few men befriend him,   fearing his strangeness;
justice demands   the gibbet for one man,
then ravens visit him,   his viscera feed them;
the fierceness of fire   finishes many;
one man at his mead,   mouthing imprudently,
falls in a brawl,   a bright blade quietens him;
one, of a surfeit   supped at the beer-benches,
ends life in misery,   mindless, a self-slayer;
one man is fortunate,   finds joy early,
the company of kinsmen   comforts his dotage.

Thus men are ruled   by a random Weird:

one is regaled   with riches and youthfulness;
one, a warrior,   on the war-field is honoured;
one at the gaming-board   gains a great fortune;
a scholar is wealthy   in wisdom and intellect;
one is gifted   in the goldsmith's art,
adorns the corslet   of a king who gratefully
rewards him richly   with realms of his own;
one brews liquor   to lighten men's burden –
is hailed as a hero   and highly respected;
one procures patronage   plundering the word-hoard,
his skill in singing   is sought-after, paid for;

one becomes famed   as a falconer, taming
the wild hawk's spirit,   he speaks to it, feeds it,
its foot in a jess,   it gently succumbs . . .

Divers are the destinies   dealt out by Fate to us.

OVIDIAN

Aeolus stilled the winds, and the dawn star
    rose up refulgent
ushering mortals to get to their business.
    Perseus, rising,
put on his swift-winged sandals and with his
    hooked sword ascended,
cleaving the clear air, leaving behind him
    numerous nations,
coming at last to Cepheus' kingdom.
    Here was Andromeda,
unjustly fettered to pay for the heinous
    crime of her mother
[Cassiopeia (Cepheus' wife) had
    angered Neptune,
boasting herself more beautiful than his
    Nereid maidens].

Perseus saw her, chain-bound there to the
    sea-battered cliff-face,
would have assumed her an alabaster
    monument, but that
hair from her forehead stirred in the wind and
    tears from her eyes welled.
Then he fell deeply besotted in love with her,
    stunned by her beauty –
almost forgetting to ply his heels' pinions,
    such was his wonder.
Landing, he cried: 'You shouldn't be bound in
    chains made of metal;
rather, the links that bond lovers should be
    yours.' And he asked her
what was her name and her nation, and the
    reason she suffered.
Being a virgin, she wouldn't presume to
    speak to a stranger,

modestly would have hidden her face in her
  hands, had they been free.
Freely, however, her eyes shed tears as
  Perseus persisted.
Then, lest her silence might seem to imply some
  culpable conduct,
hapless Andromeda told him her name and
  that of her nation,
how she was fettered unjustly for the
  crime of her mother,
there to endure an ocean monster's
  molestations.

While she was speaking the waters roared and,
  breasting the broad waves,
out of the dolorous deep advanced a
  menacing ogre.
Shrilly she screamed. Her father and mother
  (more so the latter)
each felt an impotent wretchedness, only
  able to wail grief,
clinging the while to the chained girl, making
  loud lamentations.
Perseus then addressed them: 'The time for
  grief is unending;
time for actively helping, however, is
  dreadfully short-lived.
If I were now to tell you that I am
  Perseus, son of
Danae and Jupiter, Perseus who slew the
  serpent-haired Gorgon,
Perseus who dared to brave the winds on
  feathery pinions,
then I should prove myself eligible to
  marry your daughter.
If I now add to these credentials
  that of my service

(should the gods favour me), surely you'll have to
    give me your blessing.'
This they agreed (in addition, a dowry) –
    who could refuse it?

Then, as the beak of a galley, driven
    hard by her oarsmen,
furrows the foam, so the monster's sternum
    parted the water.
Now it was only a stone's throw from where they
    stood at the cliff-base.
Suddenly Perseus sprung from the earth, rose
    up to the high clouds.
Seeing his shadow traversing the sea, the
    monster attacked it.
Just as an eagle, sighting a basking
    snake in a sunned field,
stoops on the scaled neck, deeply embedding
    dagger-sharp talons
lest the infuriated reptile
    twists its fangs backwards,
so, swooping swiftly, Perseus burst through the
    air in a steep dive,
buried his sword to the hilt in the monster's
    bellowing body.
Goaded, enraged by the wound, the brute thrashed
    rearing and plunging,
spinning around like the fierce wild boar when
    baying hounds bait it.
Deftly avoiding the greedily snapping
    maw of the monster,
plying his pinions, the hero struck its
    barnacled hump-back,
thrusting his curved blade deep in its ribs and
    slashing the finned tail.
Spray from the gushes of purple vomit
    spewed by the monster

spattered the wings of Perseus, made them
  heavy with blood spume.
Fearing to trust these gore-drenched pinions
  further, the hero
reached for a rock projecting above the
  wind-lashed surface.
Bracing himself, he firmly gripped this
  crag with his left hand,
thrusting his blade with his right hand repeatedly
  into the beast's guts —
Olympus itself, as well as the common
  people, applauded.

Cassiopeia and Cepheus, joyous,
  lauded the hero,
calling him son-in-law, saying he'd saved their
  house from destruction.
Unchained, the reason/reward for this feat of
  daring descended;
meanwhile the victor cleansed his hands in the
  brine which they brought him.
So that Medusa's snake-haired head might
  suffer no damage,
thickly he laid down leaves on the ground and
  over them seaweed,
placing the head of the Gorgon on top of them.
  Living, absorbent,
freshly-gathered, the seaweed fronds turned
  stony and brittle —
just as today all corals retain this
  quality, pliant
under the water but petrifying when
  brought to the surface.

Perseus then built altars of turf to
  honour three godheads:
one to Minerva, on which a cow was
  sacrificed duly;

next he dispatched a calf in homage to
    wing-footed Mercury;
finally, slaying a bull, he elicited
    Jupiter's favour.
Claiming Andromeda now as his prize for so
    worthy an exploit,
Perseus sought no more dowry, but straightway
    moved to the feast where
Cupid and Hymen presided fuelling
    fires with rich incense.
Garlands festooned the roof-tree; joyful
    harps and flutes sounded;
huge folding doors flung back to reveal a great
    golden interior;
sumptuous then was the banquet laid for
    Cepheus' courtiers.

When it was finished and all had indulged in
    Bacchic cavortings,
Perseus asked his hosts about local
    customs and manners.
One of them answered him, adding: 'Now tell us,
    valiant Perseus,
how you beheaded the Gorgon Medusa.' The
    hero explained how
under cold Atlas there was a place whose
    entrance was guarded
closely by two hag sisters who shared one
    eyeball between them;
while it was being transferred from one to the
    other, he stole it,
then travelled far through trackless rock-strewn
    forests, arriving
finally where the Gorgons dwelt – on
    all sides around him,
petrified beasts and men, all changed by
    glimpsing Medusa.

He hadn't looked direct in her face but had
   rather observed her
safely by way of the image reflected
   bright in his bronze shield.
She and her snakes were asleep when he severed her
   head from her shoulders;
fleet-winged Pegasus and his brother were
   born from her spilt blood.

Further, the hero told of more dangers
   bravely encountered:
oceans and lands he had witnessed, even
   stars he had soared to,
bold on his beating wings. When he had finished,
   still they were eager –
one of his hearers asked why, of all the
   Gorgon sisters,
only Medusa had tresses of coiling
   hideous serpents.
'Since what you ask is of interest to all men,
   I will inform you.
She was once famed for her loveliness, sought by
   passionate suitors,
fairest of all her attributes was her
   hair (I was told this
thing by a man I once met who claimed to have
   seen her in those days).
Neptune, however, ravished the maid in
   Minerva's temple,
whereupon modest Minerva hid her
   face with her aegis,
punished the Gorgon by changing her locks to these
   writhing reptiles.
Now, on her corslet, Minerva still wears the
   likeness of serpents;
still, on the goddess's breastplate are etched these
   terrible emblems.'

SUBMISSION

Woken by intermittent gentle
punch-like sensation left of sternum.
Fleeting consideration of summoning
medical aid rejected (incurious
  as to the Faculty's prognosis),
   seeking instead to leave a cleared desk:
    hasty addressing of this composed brief
final submission; inconsequentially
marking a page (Defoe on the Pestilence).

[. . . poor dispairing Creatures, who had the Distemper upon
them, and were grown stupid, or melancholly by their
Misery, as many were, wandred away into the Fields, and
Woods, and into secret uncouth Places, almost any where to
creep into a Bush, or Hedge, and DIE.]

PESTILENTIAL

The Country People adjacent do in Pity
carry them Food and set it at a Distance;
next Time they go, they find the Wretches dead,
the Food untouch'd.

          Then they do dig a Hole
at a great Distance, then with long Poles and Hooks
drag the dead Bodys into the dug Pits,
coming to Wind-ward that the Bodys' Scents
might blow from them; and Many do go out thus.

               *

Blind Piper was an ignorant weak poor Man
and walked his Rounds about 10 a Clock at Night
piping from Door to Door. Folk took him in
at Public Houses, plied him with Drink and Victuals
and sometimes Farthings; he in Return would pipe
and sing.

          One Night, poor Fellow, in Coleman-street,
and having a Bellyfull, laid on a Wall
and fell a sleep, when Neighbours, seeing him thus,
and hearing the Bell Man, thought him but a Corse
and plac'd a Body truly dead beside him.
The Tumbrill took both Bodys up and shot them
into the Pit – tho' Piper was but drunk.

               *

Soloman Eagle, an Enthusiast,
sallies abroad quite naked with a Pan
of burning Charcoal on his Head, denouncing
of Judgement upon the City; tho' he himself
is not at all infected, but in his Head.

THUCYDIDEAN

Continents then were affected by violent
    earthquakes, eclipses,
withering droughts and subsequent famines,
    pestilent outbreaks . . .
Faced with the Plague, the ignorant Faculty
    shewed itself impotent;
equally useless were all of our sciences,
    oracles, arts, prayers . . .
Burning sensations occurred in our heads, our
    eyes became bloodshot,
inside our mouths there was bleeding from throat and
    tongue, we grew breathless,
coughing and retching ensued, producing
    bile of all species,
genitals, fingers and toes became festered,
    diarrhoea burgeoned . . .

Terrible was the despair into which all
    fell when they realized
fully the weight and the magnitude of their
    diresome affliction . . .
Not enough living to bury the dead or
    cover the corpses . . .
Seeing how swift and abrupt were the changes
    Fortune allotted
(money and life alike being transient
    under the Pestilence),
profligate wretched citizens turned to
    lawless dishonour,
heedless of gods and of law for they thought themselves
    already sentenced –
then was there bloody and slaughterous civil
    mass insurrection.

ST LAURENCE'S

It used to be OK, indeed beneficial,
to sit for half-an-hour in April sun
on, say, the bench 'Placed here by Colonel Everett,
D.S.O./R.E., 1887
– 1963', but now it's not.

Only *naïfs* and reckless oldies loiter
(cataracts and skin-cancers burgeoning)
in the quiet precinct of St Laurence's.

REITERATIVE

[Churned out in '76,
the eroded, faded text . . .]

Cancel our dailies and monthlies:
population, energy, food,
delapse, kakistocracy,
alcoholism thriving . . .

For Western Industrial Man
this isn't just another
crisis but a climacteric . . .

This sot's liver — a metaphor
for currency's swollen decease
and Technological Man
and before him all *H. sap.*
and all that he can conceive
blown oversized by an ego
too big to survive itself
(what else, but dumbos like us,
could advocate 'More motor cars
to get us back on our feet'?) . . .

[A handful of weighed syllables
has no future (nor has Future).]

Nine out of ten oafs in the street,
a census informs us with cheer,
fondly imagine we'll find
deposits of copper and oil
ad nauseam, or find substitutes . . .
Meanwhile CIPEC and OPEC
won't *give* it away, we will pay —
or, atavistically, war . . .

As the Lifestyle Pages observe:
EARLY RETIREMENT IS COMING . . .

If ever the headlines strike home,
and they realize there's nothing to lose,
the nine out of ten will run riot –
like these on the Sports Page: terraces
dripping with apes' gore . . .

                              Yes,
add to the cumulate threats,
amassing at x to the nth,
bloody insurrection –
Homo erectus autophagous . . .

[That was in '76,
the hackneyed text is eroded,
somebody ain't been listening –
you, at the back, sit up
and fuckingwell pay attention.]

ALCMANIC

[That which remains is incongruous; frail bond
palimpsest crumbling, with it the notion;
utterance utterly lost in hiatus;
all that remains is fragmentary:] *ear-ring*

OVIDIAN

[Perseus, freeing Andromeda from her
 fetters, restored her
safe to the arms of her overjoyed father who
 offered the hero
any reward he desired – and was answered: 'The
 hand of your daughter.'
Cepheus consented (albeit she was already betrothed to
Phineus, her uncle). The marriage feast was
 duly appointed . . .]

To the assembled guests in the royal
 court of King Cepheus,
valiant Perseus was retailing deeds of
 personal prowess.
Suddenly, raucous howls of a riot
 rived the serene hall
(clearly no hymn to Hymen, but some
 presage of mayhem),
as a calm sea is whipped by a squall to
 furious breakers.

Phineus irrupted, leading the mob with a
 bronze-pointed ash-spear
(out to avenge what he saw as the theft of his
 promised Andromeda),
aimed it at Perseus, tensed for the throw, but
 Cepheus held him:
'Brother, what madness impels you to this grave
 criminal action?
It wasn't Perseus who stole your bride, but
 malicious Neptune.
Perseus saved her from being molested;
 you lacked the courage;
let him who rescued her marry her, for my
 word has been given.'

Phineus glowered at his brother and then at his
    rival, uncertain
which to attack. Then a violent spasm
    gripped the aggressor –
harmless, his flung spear splintered the bench where
    Perseus was seated.
Up leaped the hero, tugged the wedged weapon
    loose and re-launched it.
Phineus dodged it, diving behind the
    altar for cover.
Rhoetus, however, stood in the path of the
    terrible javelin,
full in the face he was struck by the bronze spike,
    sunk to the floor, felled;
when the cold metal was wrenched from his cloven
    face-bones his heels drummed,
kicking convulsively, then the spread tables were
    spattered with blood gouts.

Baying for spilt guts, the rest of the rabble
    took up their weapons,
some of them yowling that Cepheus ought to
    perish with Phineus –
Cepheus, however, had already left the
    palace, invoking
Justice and Faith and the Gods of Hospi-
    tality, saying
how he abhorred this outrage. Meanwhile,
    bellicose Pallas
flew to the aid of Perseus with the
    strength of her aegis.

There was an Indian, Athis, a handsome
    youth of just sixteen,
rich robes enhancing his beauty, a gold chain
    gracing his neck, his

ringlets, adorned with a golden headband,
  perfumed with sweet myrrh –
Athis, renowned for hurling the javelin,
  famed as an archer.
Now the boy bent his bow, Perseus seized a
  brand from the altar,
swung the still-smouldering cudgel, smashed it
  into the lovely
features; the face was instantly splattered,
  pulped into flenched mash.
Athis' lover, Lycabas, when he
  saw the boy dying,
wept for the mangled youthfulness, paused and
  snatched up the strung bow:
'Now you have me to contend with, not for
  long will you triumph
over the death of a boy whose slaying
  does you no credit –
merely arouses contempt.' And the arrow
  sped from the bowstring.
Missing its target, it lodged in the sleeve of
  Perseus' garment.
Then the great hero wielded his falchion
  (that which had severed
Gorgon Medusa's hideous head) and
  lunged into Lycabas.
Lycabas, moribund, crawled to the place where
  Athis' body
lay, and he fell there, soon to expire with
  this consolation:
even in death there is comfort through sharing,
  joined with a loved friend.

Two more, Phorbas and Amphimedon, were
  eager to join in,
slipped on the blood that flooded the floor and
  slid in the offal.

As they attempted to regain their balance
    Perseus was at them,
thrust his curved blade through the ribcage of one and the
    throat of the other.

Eurytus came next, wielding a lethal
    two-bladed battleaxe.
Perseus dispatched him by lifting a massive
    amphora (ornate,
richly embossed) and crashing it heavily
    on his opponent –
Eurytus spewed blood, fell on his back and,
    agonized, twitching,
beat his smashed head on the smirched floor. Then in
    rapid succession
Perseus slaughtered royal Polydaemon,
    Abaris, Clytus,
Lycetus, Phlegyas, Helices . . . all the while
    trampling corpses.

Phineus didn't dare tackle his foe in
    hand-to-hand combat.
Hurling his spear, he missed and struck Idas
    (who, until now, had
sided with nobody). Idas tugged out the
    javelin, snarling:
'Phineus, you force me to face you in conflict;
    you shall pay dearly.'
He was about to heave back the weapon when
    loss of blood felled him.

Hodites then was carved up by Clymenus,
    Hypseus struck down
Prothoenor, and Hypseus in turn was
    butchered by Perseus . . .

There was an old man, Emathion, who was
   just and god-fearing –
age kept him out of the fray, but his sharp tongue
   served as a weapon.
Now he stepped forward and called down a curse on
   causeless aggression.
As he was clinging with trembling hands to the
   altar, a sword-stroke
wielded by Chromis sliced off his head which
   fell on the altar,
there to exhale its last in the altar-fire,
   still execrating.

Then the twin brothers, Broteas and Ammon,
   consummate boxers
(boxing-gloves, though, are no match against cold steel),
   fell to cruel Phineus;
likewise Ampycus, a priest of Ceres.

   Standing aside was
hapless Lampetides, poet/musician,
   there for the wedding,
nervously plucking his harp-strings – the sound was
   heard by Petalus:
'Go sing the rest of your dirge to the ghosts in
   Hades!' he taunted,
driving his sword through the dome of the useless
   poet's left temple.
Groaning and twanging discordantly, he went
   down in a welter.

Irate Lycormas, avenging this outrage,
   ripped out a door-jamb,
smashed it down onto the neck of Petalus (who
   sunk like a slain bull).

One called Pelates was trying to wrench the
   jamb from the other

side, when his palm was pinned to the post by
    Corythus' flung spear,
so that he hung by his hand without falling
    when Abas slew him.

Melanus, too, a supporter of Perseus,
    died. Then Dorylas,
one of the wealthiest landowners ever,
    suffered obscenely
when he was speared through the testicles, and his
    callous assailant
commented: 'This, where you lie, is the only
    land you'll be left with.'

Perseus then, to redress this foul slaughter,
    snatched out the shaft (still
warm with the blood of Dorylas) and loosed it
    back at its owner –
in through his nose it thwacked, out through his neckbone.

    Favoured by fortune,
Perseus next slew a couple of brothers,
    Clytius and Clanis
(born of one mother – died of two different wounds):
    Clytius fell when
both of his thighs were skewered by Perseus'
    lethal flung ash-shaft;
Clanis expired with a spear down his throat, teeth
    clenched on the cold spike.

Celadon, Astreus, Aethion (this last
    noted for being
skilled in clairvoyace – albeit he failed to
    forecast his own end),
also Thoactes and infamous parri-
    cidal Agyrtes . . .
all of these fell by the spear or the blade of the
    bloodthirsty hero.

Still there remained more gratuitous violence
    on the agenda.
All the attackers were set to get Perseus,
    ganged up against him,
failed to acknowledge his valour, openly
    countered the king's pledge.
Cepheus' wife and Andromeda filled the
    hall with their shrieking
protests against this atrocity, but their
    outcries were drowned by
clashing of sword-blades and spear-tips and groans of
    agonized dying.
(All the while, blood-loving loathsome Bellona,
    goddess of warfare,
stirred up new trouble, defiling with gore the
    peace of the household.)

Phineus and his thousand supporters
    swarmed about Perseus.
Javelins flew either side of the hero
    thicker than hailstones.
Setting his back to a massive stone column he
    faced the mob's onslaught.
Molpeus led from the left and Ethemon
    rushed on the right flank.
Molpeus he stopped with a slash through the leg, then
    turned his attention
in the direction of frenzied Ethemon who
    thrust his sword wildly,
hoping to sink it in Perseus' neck but he
    struck the stone column.
Shattered, the steel bounced back at Ethemon and
    stuck in his own throat.
As he stood trembling, suppliant, Perseus
    ran his blade through him.

31

Finally, Perseus acknowledged that he was
   grossly outnumbered:
'Now you have forced me to summon the help of the
   Gorgon Medusa –
anyone here who is friendly towards me,
   now is the time to
quickly avert your eyes.' Saying which, he raised
   high the appalling
head of the Gorgon. Sceptical Thescalus
   shouldered his javelin:
'Find someone else to intimidate with your
   magical nonsense . . .'
but, as he braced to launch the shaft, he was
   petrified, static.

Ampyx came next, but his sword-thrust at Perseus
   halted in mid-stroke.
Nileus leaped forward proclaiming his greatness,
   threatening Perseus –
suddenly he was cut off in mid-speech, his
   open lips silenced.
Whereupon Eryx upbraided the warriors:
   'It's your own cowardice,
not any mystical power of a hag's head,
   makes you stand rigid!
Rush in with me and we'll overthrow this rash
   youth and his magic!'
As he raced forward he turned to a statue,
   clad in cold granite.

These all deserved the fate meted out by the
   hero; however,
one called Aconteus, Perseus' ally,
   fighting for his cause,
chanced to catch sight of the Gorgon and instantly
   froze into marble.

Thinking him still to be living, Astyages
   struck with his long sword
only to hear the steel echoing shrilly
   off the stone statue;
standing amazed, he himself was transformed to
   stone in a moment.

So many perished that listing them would be
   too time-consuming.
Only two hundred survivors remained when
   fighting had finished;
two hundred more glimpsed the head of the Gorgon and
   turned into cold stone.

Finally, Phineus regretted the conflict
   which he had started.
Seeing his statuesque forces fixed in
   various postures,
wildly he called them, touched them, incredulous
   that they were marble.
Turning away in confession of failure,
   suppliant Phineus
cried out to Perseus pleadingly, begging:
   'You are the victor!
Hide it away, that petrifying
   head of Medusa.
It wasn't hate or ambition that made me
   bear arms against you.
Why I made war was because of the woman
   I was betrothed to –
you had done more to deserve her, but I had
   known her for longer.
I am content to yield, grant me just one thing,
   greatest of heroes,
only my life.' As he babbled this plea, he
   didn't dare look up.

'Cowardly Phineus,' Perseus riposted,
  'do not be fearful.
What I can give you, I will, and don't worry,
  no sword shall hurt you.
I'll even make you a lasting memorial
  here in this palace,
so that my wife may be comforted by the
  sight of her suitor.'

Saying which, Perseus brandished the head of the
  hideous Gorgon
right in the face of the fear-stricken Phineus
  so that he saw it –
tears on his cheeks turned to stone and the craven
  cringing expression,
captured in marble, was permanent, petrified,
  pleading for mercy.

FRAGMENTARY

felled by Fate,   this fine-wrought wall.
... castle is crumbled,   constructed by giants.
Rooftrees are wrecked,   ruined towers
fester and fall.   Fate fells all.
What of the craftsmen?   Clasped in earth.
In the grave's grasp   great men perish.
Grey lichen grows   on the gore-stained stone,
the gate is mouldered,   masons of genius
bound with iron   the base of the wall ...
buildings abounded,   bath-houses, dwellings,
mead-halls were many   where men would boast,
but all was felled   by Fate's onslaught.
Pestilence came,   killing abundantly.
Those men who might   have re-made it lay dead.
What was once fought for   is wasteland now.
These courts have become   coldly bereft;
ripped from the rooftrees,   wrecked tiles lie.
... once, many men   in moods of confidence,
girt in gold,   the gear of warriors,
flushed with wine,   wealthy in silver,
counted their prized   possessions jealously ...
Stonework stood here,   a spa of water
gushed forth hotly ...

                    [Hiatus, lacuna ...
as the city is sunken   so is the word-hoard,
faded the fragile   fragment of manuscript,
parchment eroded   round the sad utterance.]

35

SHARD

As on a shard of Athenian amphora,
   summer remains fixed:
under a vine an impassioned Bacchic
   acolyte kisses,
squirting a jet of Riesling from his mouth
   into his lover's . . .

Winter: the wizened clusters cling to a
   frosted tendril,
fructose is concentrated, a honeyed
   vinous mnemonic . . .

Only one line remains of an antique
   lyrist's burden:
Sweet wine passes between the lips of
   amative partners . . .

MIDNIGHT,

> a hotel bedroom, open window,
sibilant tyres on rain-washed asphalt streets
whispering a repetitious *finish, finish*.
You stroke your lover comprehensively,
who purrs contentment, clings to your neck and sobs.
Sibilant tyres on rain-washed asphalt streets
whispering a repetitious *finish, finish*.

[UNTITLED]

A silver ear-ring,
lost last night in the hayfield,
lies in flattened grass.

EXILIC

From a lifetime of loss   this lament is compounded.
Since girlhood, no greater   grief has befallen me:
daily to suffer   the sorrow of exile,
leagues from my lover   in a land inaccessible.
Each dawn is desolate,   I desire him nightly.
Seas separate us,   sundered, I yearn for him.
Only death should divide us –   we drank to that often,
but all is altered.   Alien feelings
that he no longer   loves me as formerly
fill me with fear,   forlornly I pine here.
Lucky ones lie   lovingly together
in bed until morning;   myself, lonely,
in a fell forest   you'll find my earth-lair.
Here sobbing I sit   through summer, exiled.
Far from its haven,   my heart is storm-lashed.

VALEDICTORY

This buffer's in full retreat,
had more than enough, wants out,
can't hack the hassle, the horseshit,
the bozos on mountain bikes,
the user-hostile high-tech,
the esoteric subculture
where 'The Gorgs plant binoony berries
which the Fraggles just can't stand!',
where 'T-Bag meets Dr Strangebag
and rapidly goes off fish!',
where each successive bulletin
is more wacky, sad, obscene . . .
This buffer's had more than enough,
wants out, is in full retreat.

IDYLLIC

Chambré, decanted, '34 port (Tuke
  Holdsworth) – the stopper
carefully sealed for conveying by rucksack
  into an idyll.

[Two bushes grafted together, olive with
  wild oleaster,
through which the rain-laden wind could never
  penetrate coldly,
nor did the sun ever pierce them with shafts of
  radiant noon heat.
Crawling beneath them he gathered together a
  litter of leafmould,
lay down at last in the midst of the leaves and
  piled them around him.
Whereat Athene covered his eyelids,
  soon to release him
out of his weary exhaustion, benignly
  easing with sweet sleep.]

Thirty secured in a little brown bottle
  after a month of
(bogus insomnia) locum's prescriptions,
  comforting rattle . . .

Distant a fortnight (a farmer's *frisson*,
  finding corrupt flesh),
distant a valley (nearest point of
  vehicular access),

kingfisher-blue pulsating strobe and
  bray of the tumbril.

AUGUST:

          the steady thresh
of an advancing harvester;
the dark swift departing;
ash in Ludlow church,
HIC IACET A.E.H.;
last light is pressing the panes;
les lauriers sont coupés.

Eh OS I E

crackle   f brittle
                anhyd u^s laurel av
rustle of old   es
wizened anhydr tous scrivenings,
                 ail wisps of laurel
  half-hidden   leaves,
                glimpsed sorrowful
  parchment r   utterance
                     and the
                          sad utterance
  sepia faded
  pages of fade lous holograph

sepia-scriven psest hi roglyphs

rotted the frai mbled eroded leaves
            bond, with it the
                          utterance
                                    ,

43

Nothing For Anyone

Cancel out Dailies and Monthlies.

Population, Energy, Food
The present United Nations
Forecast of Population
for Year 2000 is over
7000 millions.*
Sadly [...] spells it out for us*
(Encounter, March [...]
for Western Industrial Man
[...] just another
crisis but a climacteric.

[...] weighty Sunday Sup.
[...]ports of alcoholism

The Art Correspondent, clearly,
don't know his Arp from his Albers:

In Sex, I read there are more
[...] stock broker's
[...] than anywhere [...]

The sot's liver a meta[...]
Sterling's swollen decline
and its chronological Man
and before him Roman, Mayan,
[...] all homo erectus
[...] he conceives as cosmos
in his own petty perspective
shown oversize by an ego
too big to survive itself.
(What about dummies like us
could ask for 'More motor cars
to put us back on our feet'?)

* A Second Look at Doom, by Sir Ashby Counter, Vol XLVI No [...]

...on velling (all reviews etse.
...mpared with De Witts Black H..es,
...al unweighed will les
...e future (nor has future).

...DEFIE ONE HUNDRED TODAY,
...THFUL ES HIS FITNESS TO..Y —
LIFE-DRUG KNOWN ONLY TO HIM!
...re unde... Ferret
in ...ole...'s *Lancer Greaves*
... this ...re Elix.. .. Long Life,
if p... ...used, will protract
...ur days ...ll you s....l h... seen
...ur count........... Of course
it will ...tak.. us by sur.rise —
...he .... in the street,
...ensu.........m ......e witt cheer,
...lly ....ll find
deposi......... oper and oil
ad...u.............r ...nds .il ...titl.es.
Pos...... pos ib. .not. —
...Me...while ..IPE. and C.... ...
...n't *give .... away*, ...e will ....y —
...t, ...avistically;

As t... Leis..re .'age. obser..
...ARE. .RE .REME.. IS C...NG.

...n reelins ....
...ried a civil a ..ipload. —
...a. sa.. .....k to he ...f,
...es. ...dd '..he cur. a...... .ats,
...uuck i...es...ed .ee ...y C.cile De Witt and   S. De Witt
Breach. ....

...N... ...io vi... p.c.
...rankl... ....e ... ...on't a... ...ese